GREENHOUSE GROWING FOR BEGINNERS

HOW TO GROW VEGETABLES AND FLOWERS

BY BEVERLY HILL

Introduction

I want to thank you and congratulate you for choosing the book, *"GREENHOUSE GROWING FOR BEGINNERS: How to Grow Vegetables and Flowers"*.

Gardening is a hobby enjoyed by millions of people throughout the world. One common drawback with traditional outdoor gardening, however, is that you are only able to grow what Mother Nature allows. Changing weather and temperatures through the seasons prohibits growing of your favorite vegetables and flowers all year long. The perfect solution for this dilemma is greenhouse gardening. Greenhouse gardening for beginners is really quite simple once you have purchased and set up your greenhouse.

Anyone who can garden in their backyard can transition to gardening in a greenhouse. Greenhouse gardening offers many advantages, including being able to grow all year long, keeping favorite plants alive all through the winter, and starting seeds more easily. You must purchase special equipment, and apply certain methods to garden successfully in a greenhouse, but they are well worth the effort.

Thanks again for choosing this book, I hope you enjoy it!

ABOUT THE AUTHOR

Beverly Hill is a sociologist. She is the CEO of C.E.F Associates and formerly served as head of department of sociology in Premier Natural Resources Inc.

A graduate of Nelson High School also graduated from the University of Toronto with a B.A in economics and finance and holds an M.S from Cambridge University in public relations and PhD in sociology.

She has written many articles on human equality, animal rights, environmental issues, personal development and peace keeping in different newspapers. She has also appeared in many magazines and is frequently interviewed for articles on family, race, socioeconomic status, and how to survive in your environment. She has also worked on the importance of health of relationship between parents and children. Her book 'The Middle Child' focuses on the importance of the attention given to the children and what to expect from them. This book helps parents understand their children.

In addition to these works she is also the author of 'Surviving Alone ' which is about her own childhood growing up; she writes about her family struggles living on a low income budget and growing her own food to survive.

C.E.F Associates formed in 1999 in Idaho, USA she worked both nationally and internationally. This is a consulting company which has clients all over the world. Ms. Hill the CEO of the company is the main reason of the huge client base because of her servings in foreign countries.

TABLE OF CONTENT

Chapter 1

GREENHOUSE GARDENING

Your greenhouse is already equipped to provide the basic necessities of light and warmth; however, there are a few additional resources that you will need to supply. As water is crucial to plant growth, you will need to set up a watering system, or make sure that a water source is easily accessible. You will also need to ensure that your greenhouse is equipped with proper ventilation. Furthermore, if you plan to grow plants all year long, you may need to set up additional heaters and artificial lights for winter days when natural sunlight is not enough.

To ensure that your plants are thriving, you need to maintain a steady temperature of around 80 degrees. Heaters will be needed to achieve this temperature during the winter months, but during early spring and fall it is possible to achieve steady temperatures without incurring additional heating cost. One great tip for beginners is to fill a few dark painted gallon containers with water, and place them inside your greenhouse in areas that will receive direct sunlight. In setting up your greenhouse, you will need to do some research on the plants you intend to grow to make sure they are each placed in the best spot.

A trip to your local gardening center will often provide all the information you need as their employees are often knowledgeable on different types of plants, and their required growing conditions. Another important tip for beginning gardeners is to store all fertilizers and chemicals away from your greenhouse. Being exposed to the moisture in a greenhouse can cause some chemicals to evaporate into the air which can damage your plants, and be dangerous for your health.

A greenhouse can be a great asset when starting seeds, or growing vegetables in your garden, it extends the growing season, and can provide you with fresh vegetables through the winter and early spring. Successful vegetable growing requires the right environment in your greenhouse. Environmental elements to be considered are heat in cold months, cooling in warm months, ventilation & air circulation, shading, humidity, lighting, and more.

Chapter 2

STARTING SEEDS/HEATING/LIGHTING

Seed starting for the summer or winter vegetable garden is a very common use for a greenhouse. With a greenhouse, you can get an early start to your garden, or even have vegetables year round. Needed seed starting supplies are containers, sterile soil, fertilizer, water, and especially for northern gardeners, heat and light. A relatively inexpensive way to start seeds is using a propagation mat under seed flats. This provides warmth directly to the soil to help with germination. An alternative to using flats is to plant seeds directly into a soil bench. Warmth can be provided with a heat cable buried about 6 inches in the soil.

HEATING

Heating the greenhouse can be provided with electric, natural gas, or LP gas heaters. Electric heaters are flexible, economical, and easy to install with 240-volt heaters generally being more efficient than 120 volt. However, a 120-volt heater is usually adequate for heating a small greenhouse when controlled by a separate heavy-duty, moisture resistant thermostat. Natural gas and LP heathers should be properly vented, both providing fresh air for combustion, and exhausting fumes, and equipped with a good thermostat. Other less common heating methods include in-the-floor radiant heating or an extension of a forced-air home heating system to an attached greenhouse.

LIGHTING

Once the seeds come up they need light. If the natural light in your greenhouse is low (a common issue in winter), providing supplemental lighting is important to keep plants from getting spindly. A simple fluorescent shop light hung about 4 inches above your plants may be enough. However, many growers prefer to use High Output Fluorescent lamps, High Pressure Sodium, Mental Halide, or LED grow lights. These specialized lights provide strong, full spectrum light, and can often cover a larger area than ordinary fluorescent. The high output fluorescent lamps and LED grow lights are energy efficient as well.

Chapter 3

VEGATABLES TO GROW IN THE WINTER GREENHOUSE

Vegetables commonly grown in a winter greenhouse include lettuce, spinach, radishes, tomatoes, peppers, and cucumbers. However, what you are actually able to successfully grow depends on the nighttime temperatures you decide to keep. A cool greenhouse, with nighttime temperatures of 40-45degrees F, works for lettuce, spinach and radishes. Peppers, tomatoes, and cucumbers need warmer temperatures at night, around 65degreeF, especially when fruit is growing.

POLLINATION

Vegetables growing in a greenhouse often need help with pollination. Standard cucumbers will need hand pollination, taking the male blossom, and gently rubbing the female blossom center. Tomatoes and peppers are self-pollinating, but the blossoms should be gently shaken, or vibrated on a regular basic. Circulation fans can help move plants. A preferred alternative is to look in a seed catalogs for varieties of seeds that are appropriate for greenhouse production, often due to their method of pollination.

WATERING

Water is needed, but the amount and frequency varies with temperatures, day length, plant size, and your growing medium. It is recommended that the plants be soaked thoroughly at every watering. In January, watering may be needed every 10 to 14 days. As the days get warmer, the frequency should be increased. A flat of seedlings being warmed by a heat mat will also dry out more quickly. When watering, avoid splashing foliage to prevent spreading diseases.

VENTILATION

In the winter, it can be difficult to prevent the growth of mold and mildew. Do not over water. and help control humidity with proper ventilation and air circulation. For air circulation I recommend an oscillating fan running 24/7 all year long. For ventilation in the warmer months, the gentlest form of ventilation is through natural convection with base wall vents. or jalousie (louvered) windows pulling cool air in down low, with roof vents allowing hot air out through the roof.

COOLING

Positive cooling is usually not needed in a greenhouse as long as adequate humidity and shading is provided on hot days. If positive cooling is needed, I suggest using evaporative air coolers, which humidify as they cool. Air conditioners are not good for plants since they remove moisture from the air.

Chapter 4

THE IMPORTANCE OF THE GREENHOUSE EFFECT

One of the factors that affect the world's environmental conditions is the greenhouse effect. Climate scientists often blame the greenhouse effect for contributing to Earth's environmental woes, but it has a vital positive effect on the planet as well. Without this atmospheric condition, life on Earth would be vastly different, or even nonexistent.

THE GREENHOUSE EFFECT

The greenhouse effect refers to the ability of the atmosphere to trap the sun's heat, increasing the temperature of the planet. When the sun's energy reaches Earth, that atmosphere absorbs some of it on the way down, and then absorbs more when the energy reflects back of the surface during the day. This trapped energy heats up the atmosphere, increasing the temperature of the planet, and distributing warmth to its night side, when solar heating is unavailable. The denser the atmosphere, and the higher the concentration of energy-holding molecules like water vapor and carbon dioxide, the more energy the atmosphere can trap.

POSITIVE EFFECTS

The greenhouse effect is important, because it contributes to the survival of life on Earth. Without the greenhouse effect, the temperature of the planet would be similar to conditions experienced on the moon. On the lunar surface, with no atmosphere to mediate temperature swings, the surface can reach 134 degrees Celsius (273 degrees Fahrenheit) during the day, and -153 degrees Celsius (-244 degrees Fahrenheit) at night. This dramatic temperature change required NASA to develop specialized gear to protect astronauts from both extremes for the moon landings. A similar temperature swing on Earth would have produced an environment hostile to most living things.

TOO MUCH OF A GOOD THING

Unfortunately, while a moderate greenhouse effect is vital to life, an elevated greenhouse effect can be dangerous. Since the Industrial Revolution, the widespread adoption of fossil fuels has increased the amount of carbon dioxide, water vapor, and other greenhouse gases in the atmosphere. According to a study by the Carbon Dioxide Information Analysis Center of the United States Department of Energy, carbon dioxide level have increased 39.5 percent since 1750, while levels of methane in the atmosphere have jumped by 150 percent. Climate scientists point to this increase in heat-trapping gases as one of the reasons global temperatures have risen during this period.

EXTREME EFFECTS

One of the chief concerns about an increase in the greenhouse effect is that the changes can become self-sustaining. As more greenhouse gases enter the atmosphere, its ability to trap heat increases. As the warmth of the atmosphere increases the amount of water vapor it can hold increases as well, further boosting the effect. In addition, increased global temperatures threaten to release large amounts of carbon that is currently frozen into permafrost zones, also exacerbating the problem. Excessive heat retention could lead to massive changes in natural water distribution, and available land mass on a global scale. The effect of mitigating factors, such as, increased cloud cover reflecting sunlight back into space, is not well understood.

Chapter 5

HOW TO GROW VEGETABLES AND FLOWERS

There's a bit of fabulous chaos happening in the gardening world. Beans are happily climbing with clematis. Herbs are cohabitating with Echinacea. Food is growing with flowers.

It used to be that vegetable gardens were stuck in an out-of-sight corner of the backyard, and flower gardens occupied the high profile spaces around our homes. Not anymore. Plants are busting out of their traditional roles, and growing together-wherever-in harmony.

We've been boxing things up too much, said horticulturalist Erica Shaffer. "Why do we have to have a perennial garden or vegetable garden? Why can't we just GARDEN?" This isn't a new idea. For centuries the French have had formal decorative and functional vegetable gardens. In medieval times, wealthy Englishmen added herbs and flowers to their kitchen gardens.

Inter-planting flowers and vegetable does more than pretty-up the veggie patch. Integrating flowers into your vegetable gardens, or growing vegetables in with your flower borders can be fun and beneficial.

Pollinating insects like butterflies and bees are crucial for vegetable development. With squash, for instance, you can have lush vines and leaves topped off with stellar large flowers, but if those flowers aren't pollinated, no squash will develop. Beneficial insects are also important because they target and organically control many pests, like the tomato hornworm for example.

Shaffer also says, adding flowers and herbs to your garden, repels some pests, while I have yet to see a nose on an insect. Mixing flowers and herbs up with vegetables confuses critters. Different smells camouflage each other, and fewer pests are drawn to your garden, she said. As interest in growing our own food increases, many gardeners are adding vegetables to their borders and flower gardens. Vegetable plants rival ornamental plants in their beauty. Delicate white snap pea blossoms sit on top butterfly-shaped leaves as wispy tendrils curl and dance. There's added benefit in that pea tendrils are edible, and an attractive addition to salads.

Exotic looking kale with tall, sturdy, yet ruffled leaves could substitute for elephant ear, or banana in a landscape. Yet, you can't add elephant ear to a stir-fry. Kale is jammed packed with vitamins and minerals. Dill or fennel foliage is feathery and delicate. Fine foliage herbs are comparable in texture to ornamental grass, and would be perfectly at home in a perennial border.

While some veggie plants are easily seen as decorative, Shaffer says beauty is in the eye of the beholder with some veggie plants.

If you're still harvesting tomatoes in September from a plant in your front yard, maybe you won't judge the plant so harshly if it's beginning to look a little ragged. There are things to consider when adding vegetables to flower gardens. Shaffer said she would think about how many rabbits are in your neighborhood. Planting vegetable among ornamentals provides more hiding space for rabbits making it easier for them to wipe out you harvest.

It is also necessary to match vegetable, and ornamental plants with the same growing requirements. Vegetables need six or more hours of sun, and they need good soil if you aren't interested in sequentially planting vegetables in your flower beds, choose vegetables with a long growing season. Peas and some leafy greens are attractive during the cool seasons of spring and fall, don't handle heat. That might be fine in a perennial bed that fills out in the summer, but if you need summer interest, beans, corn or melons have longer growing seasons.

To keep things pretty while growing flower and food together. Shaffer suggests pondering some classic landscape design rules. Cluster plants in multiples of three of five, and vary height and textures of the plants you're choosing.

Remember that beauty is indeed in the eye of the beholder, so just garden. If growing food is the most important thing to you, express yourself and go nuts with veggie plants in your landscape. If flowers are your thing, train morning glories up your cornstalks. The most beautiful thing of all is finding your personal vision in the garden.

Chapter 6

REASONS FOR GROWING VEGETABLES

Growing vegetables at home is one of the best means to spend your free time. Vegetables are also hailed as a very good source of many types of vitamins and minerals, having them in your own lot are more than a luxury. Aside from that, you are assured that what you are eating is indeed fresh, and free from contaminants as you are the one who grew it. Freshness is maintained as you need not keep them inside your refrigerator for a long period, and you just have to get ample amount needed for the recipe you are cooking.

Growing vegetable and maintaining such is a fun and exciting activity. Although there are those who prefer to have flower gardens over this type because they think that vegetables are bland, and are better left for farmers, the truth is exactly the opposite. For those who are not yet convinced, here are the best reasons why you should start creating a vegetable plot at home.

Magnificent image of edible garden vegetables are never an eyesore. The variety of color as well as texture will never be considered second best to ornamental landscape gardens. Growing vegetables is a healthier option-although other types of gardening will give you the benefits of fresh air and exercise, but it is only by maintaining a vegetable plot that you will be provided with inorganic, and fresh vegetable for you table.

Like other plants, vegetables have flowers too-most perceive vegetables as merely patchy bland greens; striking flowers are actually blooming in the middle of the greenish plot. Although not typically observed, a number of vegetable flowers are as attractive as ornamental.

Edible plot at home will reduce cost-you will reduce your grocery budget. Therefore, instead of buying those veggies from the market whose origin you are not certain of, try to plant one at home.

Kitchen garden is versatile-as a source for many ingredients for your favorite dish, a plot could be adorned with those veggies, fruits, herbs and edible weeds that are useful in your kitchen. Having them, side-by-side in one plot is never a problem.

A green plot at home increase your friends-Once word comes around your village that you have the most attractive tomatoes in your backyard soon before you realize it you'll have neighbors visiting your home to take a look into that garden, and ask for some advice on how to grow them.

Conclusion

For any gardener who enjoys working with their plants, a greenhouse is a welcome addition to expand their hobby. Greenhouse gardening can be as intensive, or as low-key as you want it to be, depending on how much gardening you do, and how much money you want to invest in the hobby. Serious gardeners wishing to expand their interest into greenhouse gardening may opt for a permanent structure in their backyard, possible something that incorporates a cement foundation, integrated doors and windows, and an auto-venting system for temperature control.

On the other end of the spectrum, we have the beginning gardener, or hobby horticulturist who wishes to cultivate plants indoors during the winter months, or start seeds indoors in the spring for a head start on the summer growing season. This more basic form of greenhouse gardening will be our focus for this book.

Basic greenhouse gardening usually begins indoors with a temporary structure that can be set up when it's needed, and taken down when it's not. An inexpensive shelving kit will work well for this purpose, provided you have space to set it up. Other structures could be a tabletop that's not in use or an old workbench. If you are purchasing something new for the purpose of indoor gardening, look for a structure that's lightweight, and that can be easily disassembled for storage. Consider buying plastic, if you have the option, so that you can easily wipe away any dirt or water that accumulates.

Finally, if you enjoyed this book, would you be kind enough to leave a review for this book on Amazon? It'd be greatly appreciated!

Thank you again for choosing this book and good luck!

Preview Of 'GREENHOUSE: HOW TO BUILD YOUR OWN GREENHOUSE'

Chapter 1

WHAT IS A GREENHOUSE

The definition of a greenhouse also referred to as a glasshouse sometimes when you have enough heating it is also called a hot house. It's a structure made of walls and roof which is designed or built with transparent materials like glass, and in this structure we have plants (not just any plants but plants requiring controlled climatic conditions) grown within such structure, hence the name Greenhouse is derived from this kind of setting.

The environmental benefits of having a greenhouse is so immense, because of the alarming environmental situation of the world today, especially the problem of global warming, air pollution and all manner of pollution experienced in the environment which we live it really warrants us to start thinking about having a greenhouse. To have a greenhouse is not difficult as some people many think. The materials range in size from small or medium size sheds to much more industrial bigger sized building materials.

GREENHOUSE

HOW TO BUILD YOUR OWN GREENHOUSE

BEVERLY HILL

Go to Amazon.com to read the rest of "**GREENHOUSE: HOW TO BUILD YOUR OWN GREEN**"

BONUS: SUBSCRIBE TO THE FREE BOOK

Beginners Guide to Yoga & Meditation

"Stressed out? Do You Feel Like The World Is Crashing Down Around You? Want To Take A Vacation That Will Relax Your Mind, Body And Spirit? Well this Easy To Read Step By Step

E-Book Makes It All Possible!"

Instructions on how to join our mailing list, and receive a free copy of "Yoga and Meditation" can be found in any of my Kindle eBooks.

NOTES

NOTES

NOTES

NOTES

NOTES

28160304R00018

Printed in Great Britain
by Amazon